THE EXPANDING KINGDOM

How to Unleash God's Abundance in Your Daily Life

JONATHAN BERNIS

ISBN 978-0-9798311-1-9

Jewish Voice Ministries International
US: PO Box 31998, Phoenix, AZ 85046-1998
Europe: PO Box 628, Borehamwood, WD6 9AT UK
Jewish Voice Ministries Canada
PO Box 476, Maple Ridge, BC V2X 3P2
www.jewishvoice.org

The Expanding Kingdom
How to Unleash God's
Abundance in Your
Daily Life

"Then Yeshua asked, 'What is the Kingdom of God like? What shall I compare it to? It is like a mustard seed which a man took and planted in his garden. It grew and became a tree, and the birds of the air perched in its branches.' Again he asked, 'What shall I compare the Kingdom of God to? It is like yeast that a woman took and mixed into a large amount of flour until it worked all through the dough.'" Luke 13:18-21

Much of Yeshua's teaching was done through parables. Parables use simple, visible illustrations from everyday situations to reveal the order, the nature, or the governing laws and principles of the invisible. Yeshua here is revealing a principle, a governing law about the Kingdom of God.

Now there is some ambiguity about the meaning of the phrase "the Kingdom of God." As a result, there is a lot of confusion on the part of God's people as to what the Kingdom of God is. Throughout the history of the Church, there has been a debate regarding the nature, meaning, and timing of the Kingdom of God.

This is an expression that we find often in the Scripture. And it is important for us to understand God's plan for our role as citizens of His Kingdom. Some people think the Kingdom of God is solely in the future. In other words, to them, the Kingdom of God is Heaven. It's the place we're going when we die or when He returns and takes us to Him.

But I believe that the Kingdom of God is more than just the world to come. While I don't believe that the Kingdom of God is solely in the future, it is certainly true that some of the promises of

Scripture are for days that still lie ahead. One day the Lord will rule the Earth and the lion will lie down with the lamb as the prophet Isaiah foretold. That certainly is not happening in our day!

I believe that the Kingdom of God is also in the present. It is not just something we have to long and wait for— it is meant to be a reality in our daily lives. The best definition I've heard concerning the Kingdom of God is this: "The Kingdom of God is the rule, the reign, or the manifest presence of God."

We know from the Scriptures that God is omnipresent. David said in Psalm 139:7-12:

Where can I go from your Spirit? Where can I flee from your presence?

If I go up to the heavens, you are there; if I make my bed in the depths, you are there.

If I rise on the wings of the dawn, if I settle on the far side of the sea,

even there your hand will guide me, your right hand will hold me fast.

If I say, "Surely the darkness will hide me and the light become night around me,"

even the darkness will not be dark to you; the night will shine like the day, for darkness is as light to you.

In this passage we see a beautiful presentation of the truth that God is everywhere. But there is a difference between the *omni*-presence of God, and the *manifest* presence of God. God is omnipresent, but when His Spirit is visible or tangible and we can see Him at work, then we have the manifest presence of God. And the Kingdom of God is the manifest presence, the rule, or the reign of God.

The presence of God, in the future sense of the Kingdom, is what will make Heaven be Heaven! Without the presence of God, without the rule or the reign of God, we would have no Heaven. In fact, I think Hell is best defined as simply the lack of the presence of God. The complete and total removal of God's presence is the reason there is absolute darkness and unrelieved suffering in Hell.

Heaven will be characterized by the presence of God in our midst, in a very tangible and real way. Almost no one disagrees with this aspect of the Kingdom—that it will be real in the future. But not everyone agrees that the Kingdom is also real in the present.

Let me show you from the Scriptures why I believe that the Kingdom of God is not just for our future. In Matthew 3:2 we see these words, "Repent, for the Kingdom of God is at hand." Literally, the phrase reads "the Kingdom of God is *here.*" This is a present-tense verb.

In Matthew 12:28, Yeshua said this to the Pharisees, "If I cast out demons by the spirit of God, then the Kingdom of God has come unto you." Here we see another present-tense verb.

In Luke 10:8 Yeshua says this (speaking to His disciples), "When you enter a town, eat what is set before you, heal the sick who are there and tell them 'the Kingdom of God is nigh' (or near) unto you." Again Yeshua refers to the Kingdom using the present tense.

Finally in Luke 17:20 we read, "Once

having been asked by the Pharisees when the Kingdom of God would come, Yeshua answered, 'The Kingdom of God does not come to you with careful observation, nor will people say here it is or there it is, because the Kingdom of God is within you.'" Note again the description of the Kingdom in the present tense. Yeshua does not say that the Kingdom *will be* within you, He says that it *is* within you. What is Yeshua saying here, and what does He mean?

I believe He is saying the rule, the reign, and the presence of God is within you right now. How does that impact our daily lives? When Yeshua says in Matthew 6:33, "Seek ye first the Kingdom of God and His righteousness," He is saying, "Seek ye first the rule of God, seek ye first the reign of God, seek ye first the manifest presence of God, and everything else will be added unto you. Seek ye first the dominion of God in your life and the lives of those around you, and everything else will fall into place." Yeshua is telling us how to live a Kingdom life in the present.

In our parable, Yeshua said the Kingdom of God (the rule, or the reign, or the manifestation of the presence of God) is like a mustard seed growing into a tree and like yeast put into flour spreading throughout the dough. What is Yeshua teaching through these illustrations? What is the principle here? What are we being told about the Kingdom of God?

To answer those questions, we need to ask another: What do these two things, the mustard seed and the yeast, have in common? Both produce *expansion*. Both produce *growth*. The seed, after being planted in the ground, will grow into a very large plant. After the yeast is mixed into the dough, it rises...it expands.

The Kingdom of God Is Perpetually Expanding

What Yeshua is saying here, and this is such an important principle that we all need to get into our spirits, is that the nature of the Kingdom of God, the nature of the rule or the reign of God, the order of the Kingdom of God, is perpetual expansion. God's Kingdom plan for your life involves expansion and blessing.

We see this point illustrated throughout Scripture. When God created Adam and Eve, He told them to, "Be fruitful and multiply." (Gen. 1:28) That's part of the Adamic Covenant. That was their mission. That was their purpose. That was their call.

Adam and Eve were to be fruitful and multiply, take dominion over the Earth and subdue it. That assignment illustrates for us the expanding nature of the Kingdom of God. From the very beginning of creation, God's plan was for growth and increase. Let me give you another example.

God spoke to Abraham, and He said, "Leave your family and your country, and I will make your family like the stars of Heaven, like the sand of the shores, and all the countries of the Earth will be blessed through you." (Gen. 12:1-3) What was God's plan for Abraham's life? Expansion. Growth.

Listen to what Yeshua Himself said to His disciples, "But I, when I be lifted up from the Earth, will draw all men unto me." He also said this, "Except a corn of wheat fall to the ground and die, it abideth alone. But if it dies, it brings forth much fruit." (John 12:24) What is the principle He is teaching? Expansion!

Most varieties of corn have two or three ears per stalk. On average, an ear of corn will have about 800 kernels. So from just one kernel planted in the ground, the harvest can be 1600 to 2400 kernels of corn! That is the way God's Kingdom works. And that is His plan for your life.

Just before He returned to Heaven, Yeshua told His disciples, "But you will receive power when the Holy Spirit comes on you and you will be my witnesses in Jerusalem, Judea and Samaria, and the uttermost ends of the Earth." (Acts 1:8) Why did He tell them that? Because the nature of the Kingdom of God, the principle of God's rule and reign, not just in the future but right now in our lives today, is continual growth and expansion.

Let me repeat this again, because it is so important for you to get this truth into your spirit. The nature of the Kingdom of God, the very nature of God's rule and reign, is growth and expansion.

One of the best-known prophecies in the Old Testament concerning the Messiah is Isaiah 9:6 which says, "Unto us a child is born, unto us a son is given, and his name shall be called Wonderful, Counsellor, Mighty God, Everlasting Father, Prince of Peace." The very next verse, verse 7 says, "Of the increase of His government and peace there will be no end."

Because death and sin are a part of our world, the natural order is decay, decomposition, and breakdown. What a contrast to God's Kingdom plan of growth and increase! And remember that God means for you to be living in His Kingdom today.

Decay is what always happens without the presence and reign of God. What happens in a society that turns its back on God? That society decays. Just look at the nations around the world today. The political, economic, and social arenas are scarred by the failures of men and women who have refused to acknowledge the Kingdom of God.

The nature of God's Kingdom, on the other hand is life, growth, and expansion. When God is ruling, when God is reigning, when God is present there is always life and there is always growth. Amen!

It's interesting in considering this principle that salvation works the same way. If you read the Scriptures carefully, you'll see that salvation is both past, present, and future tense. For example 1st Corinthians 1:18 says, "For the message of the cross is foolishness to those that are perishing," present tense, "but to us who are being saved," present tense, "it is the power of God."

I heard this once, and I think it's great. We were saved, past tense, from the penalty of sin; we are being saved, present tense, from the power of sin; and we shall be saved, future tense, from the presence of sin. I think it's a very true statement.

The present tense of salvation, that we are being saved from the power of sin in our lives, is actually the expansion of God's rule and reign in our lives. Let me give you an example from my own life and testimony that illustrates this principle of expansion in the life of a believer:

When I accepted the Lord in a Bible study years ago, I had no idea what I was getting into. And it's been quite a different life than anything I ever expected. My goal in life had been to make my million, two million, three million by the time I was thirty, and be an international financier.

I've come close to that a few years ago when I was living in Russia in a one bedroom apartment! Not really! But anyway: I've been rich in the spirit. Hallelujah! But when I made my decision to follow Yeshua, I really had no idea what I was doing or where God would take my life.

The first thing that happened to me about three days later is that I had an overwhelming urge to read the Scriptures. No matter what I did, I could not shake it! So I looked everywhere for a Bible, but I couldn't find one. I really had no idea where to get one, but I knew I couldn't go to the synagogue. I didn't even have a friend who owned a Bible. I was so far removed from spiritual things that I had no idea at the time that the Bible was the bestselling book of all time, and I could go to any bookstore and find a copy.

So I drove all the way back to Rochester, New York from Buffalo, 60 miles on my motorcycle, and dug through every box until I found a Bible that someone had given me back in high school. And I began to devour the Bible. I would read and read, and the Word of God began to do its work in my heart.

After a couple of weeks of reading the Word, something else changed. Now don't hold this against me, it was a long, long time ago, but I was quite an experimenter in those days. I was what we called an "unlicensed pharmacist." That's the term that we used. Of course it was all experimental!

To give you some idea of where I was when I got saved, my idea of going cold turkey was cutting down to just smoking pot. Pot wasn't really a drug for me after two years of college; it was just part of normal life. But as I read the Word, I started to feel this desire to remove myself from all the drugs. My heart's desire became to just get rid of all the drugs and to walk free from addiction.

To be honest with you, when I first started contemplating getting off drugs, I didn't think I could do it. I still vividly remember sitting out on my porch, playing the guitar and praising the Lord. I later found as I studied more of the Scripture that I was singing Psalms that I didn't even know existed. The words were just coming out of my mouth. And it was like I heard the Lord say, "You don't need those drugs anymore." At that moment it was like my chains fell off. I was instantly freed from the drugs. Praise God. His

Kingdom was growing in my life.

I remember we used to have gourmet meals in college. (I'm just confessing all sorts of things here!) We would go to a large grocery store. We would pay for the bread and the eggs, and the inexpensive things. But as we walked through the store, we would get jumbo shrimp (forgive me Lord!) and eat them as we walked down the aisle. We were eating a gourmet shrimp cocktail meal— for free.

And I remember going to the store about a week after I was saved, and without really thinking about it, I threw a can of macadamia nuts into my pocket and got some shrimp. That was normal for me. After all the store was making a profit on the bread and cheese and eggs I was paying for so they could afford it— that was my mentality.

But this time as I was eating these jumbo shrimp, I got to feeling really uncomfortable about it. My problem wasn't that shrimp aren't kosher, I'd been eating them for a long time without giving that a second thought. My problem was that I was stealing. And I remember driving my motorcycle out of the parking lot, and feeling a tremendous sense of conviction and guilt for what I was doing. And that was the last time I ever stole.

And I look back now and see how the Kingdom of God expanded in my life. It started as a seed when I prayed a prayer, and it grew as I started to read the Bible. It was expanding to push the bondage of drug use out of my life. It was expanding into things that I had thought were okay, and pushing them out of my life. The Kingdom of God began as a seed and was expanding in me!

That's how salvation works. It starts as a prayer from our hearts, and the Word of God begins to take root, and expands in us and changes us, and molds us into the image of His Son. Paul said, "For those God foreknew he also predestined to be conformed to the likeness of his Son, that he might be the firstborn among many brothers." (Rom. 8:29) That happens as our nature is submitted to the reign, to the rule, to the manifest presence of God.

We see this principle in so many areas of the Christian life. Healing is the expansion of God's control, God's rule, God's reign, over the sickness of our body. God's Kingdom pushes the sickness out. Deliverance is the expansion of God's rule, His reign, or manifest presence over the enemy's foothold in our lives. So the principle is that the Kingdom of God is in perpetual growth and expansion, and we can choose to yield to that expanding nature, or not to yield to it.

The little boy had two fish and five loaves of bread. That's all he had. And he yielded to the Kingdom of God. He yielded to the rule, to the reign of God, to the Messiah. He gave what he had. That simple lunch of two fish and five loaves became a buffet for 5000 people, and there was a twelve basket doggie bag left over. Jesus was feeding Jewish customers, and they were happy. That's impressive!

This principle works with your finances! You take that 10%, that tithe, and you yield it to the control, to the rule, to the reign of God, and somehow, I still don't fully understand how, the 90% goes further than the 100% did before. And if you think that's good, try giving 20, 30 or 40%! There are even people who have gotten to the place where they keep 10%

and give Him 90%!

I remember when I was the Rabbi for a local synagogue. I was very concerned about how many guest speakers I would have in, because I was afraid that if we were continually asking people to give to outside works, we would have a shortage right at home. And for a long time, I did that. I controlled the number of guest speakers.

I'm not saying that leaders have to constantly have guest speakers, or special offerings every week. But as I began to learn this principle, I realized that if we gave more outside the congregation, God would meet our needs inside. The Kingdom of God is in perpetual growth, and I want to tell you that it works! The more speakers we had in, the more we gave away to other works and ministries, the more we had!

This doesn't work in the natural. It doesn't make sense. Apart from the Spirit of God, no one would believe it. But there are a lot of things that we can't understand about the Book in the natural. But it works, doesn't it? It works every time!

The Kingdom of God
Starts Small

We may have just a few little talents, but when we submit them to the rule of God and the reign of God, God expands them. Moses couldn't even talk. The disciples were just fisherman. And that shows us another principle in this parable of the Kingdom. Both of the things Yeshua used to illustrate God's Kingdom are small!

The mustard seed is tiny. The yeast is tiny. Have you ever opened a package of yeast? I tried to make bread once or twice, and I've decided that's it for me! I put in just a little tiny bit of yeast, and the whole thing just went poof! And I quickly learned that if you leave it unattended, it'll really go over the bowl, out onto the counter and make an enormous mess!

Many times we do not think we can do anything for God because we are not rich, talented, famous, or attractive. Who am I, you may ask? What do I have to offer? Guess what? People like Moses and Paul asked the same questions…and God answered by using them to change the world.

Do you remember the parable of the talents? Yeshua told of a man who gave one of his servants ten talents, one five talents, and one received one talent. Then the master left them with the responsibility to use those talents wisely. Look at what happened next.

After a long time the master of those servants returned and settled accounts with them. The man who had received the five talents brought the other five. 'Master,' he said, 'you entrusted me with five talents. See, I have gained five more.' His master replied, 'Well done, good and faithful servant! You have been faithful with a few things; I will put you in charge of many things. Come and share your master's happiness!' The man with the two talents also came. 'Master,' he said, 'you entrusted me with two talents; see, I have gained two more.' His master replied, 'Well done, good and faithful servant! You have been faithful with a few things; I will put you in charge of many things. Come and share your master's happiness!' Then the man who had received the one talent came. 'Master,' he said, 'I knew that you are a hard man, harvesting where you have not sown and gathering where you have not scattered seed. So I was afraid and went out and hid your talent in the ground. See, here is what belongs to you.' His master replied, 'You wicked, lazy servant! So you knew that I harvest where I have not sown and gather where I have not scattered seed? Well then, you should have put my money on deposit with the bankers, so that when I returned I would have received it back with interest. Take the talent from him and give it to the one who has the ten talents.' (Matt. 25:18-28)

Some people do have more talents than others. (In this parable, the talent is a measure of money, not ability, but the principle is true either way.) I want you to notice that the one talent servant was held just as accountable as the five and ten talent servants. God expects you to be faithful with whatever He has entrusted to you—even if it seems tiny.

I remember when we held our first festival in Moscow. Looking back now, I'm amazed that we had that event. I had a whole line of people telling me all the reasons it wouldn't work. I didn't have the experience or the resources to do what needed to be done. But I did know that God had called me. I told one of my friends, "We've got to go for this; the door of opportunity is closing."

We had to choose between a hall that seated 7,000 people and a stadium that seated 18,500. And I prayed and made the decision that we were going to go all out. I remember feeling so good about that decision when I made it. And I remember the first time I walked into that stadium. I felt like a mouse! That place was huge.

I started talking to myself. "Who am I?" I asked. "What have I done?" I could picture the team coming from America and seeing about 80 people in that huge stadium. The enemy brought people by to tell me all the stories of different groups that had tried and failed to fill that building. Even great preachers and evangelists had only seen tiny crowds there.

Then we started to run into

problems with the police because we were handing out literature promoting the event. I was told by a number of people, "You'll never be able to hand out this literature. The police will stop you." Well guess what? They didn't stop us. In fact, the police chief of Moscow came to our festival! Hallelujah! In fact, we brought him up on the stage and introduced him to the crowd. I'm telling you he looked impressive with the big gold bars on his uniform, and that impressive hat. God blessed us with an amazing festival.

I'll tell you that increased my faith. Why? Because little us, BIG GOD! Get it? Hallelujah! We submit little us, little yeast, little mustard seed to the rule, to the reign, to the manifest presence of God, and there's an expansion, there's a growth. God takes our little and makes it much.

Jewish Voice has now held festivals all over the world. We've been to South America, Africa, India, and across the former Soviet Union. God has blessed this ministry incredibly, and it's all because we took the little that we had and yielded it to His Kingdom.

By the way, this brings up a very important issue—numbers! I've heard some people say, "God isn't concerned about numbers. He's concerned about quality not quantity!" To listen to them, you'd think that God is looking for a few good men, just like the Marines. I was looking for a word to describe this line of thinking and the only appropriate word that came to my mind was *"STUPID!"* Forgive me for being blunt!

Think about these Scripture verses in light of that mentality: "If I be lifted up from this Earth, I'll draw a few good quality people unto me." (John 12:32) quality people unto me." (John 12:32)

"God so loved the world that He sent His only begotten Son that a few good men would believe in Him and not perish." (John 3:16) "For it is God's will that none should perish, but a few quality people should come to repentance." (2 Peter 3:9)

NO! That is not what the Word says. "And I, if I am lifted up from the earth, will draw all peoples to Myself." (John 12:32) "God so loved the world that He gave His only begotten Son, that whoever believes in Him should not perish but have everlasting life." (John 3:16) For it is not God's will that "that any should perish but that all should come to repentance." (2 Peter 3:9)

God wants both quality *and* quantity! Amen! They are NOT mutually exclusive. Numbers are important, or they wouldn't be recorded in the Bible. God wants both quality and quantity in our movement and in His Kingdom.

God's Kingdom Needs the Right Environment to Expand

There is one more principle about the Kingdom of God that we see illustrated for us in the parable Yeshua told. The yeast has to be added to the bread in order for it to expand. The mustard seed has to be planted in the ground in order to grow.

What's the point? They must be in the right environment, or no expansion will occur. Remember what I told you about my bread-making exploits? I didn't use (quite) all the yeast in making my dough. The part that I didn't use sat in the jar and never made a mess on the counter. The yeast needed to be taken out and used before it could expand.

God spoke to me on an airplane in 1992, and He said, "Go to St. Petersburg and reach My people." At that time, I had no idea about the festivals and how God would use them to reach His Chosen

People around the world. The details of that first festival were revealed only after I went to St. Petersburg. The seed has to be planted in the right place. The yeast has to be released to the bread.

If I had sat back and waited until I knew all of the details, none of these great festivals would ever have happened. I had to take the little that I had—the small seed, the tiny yeast—and yield it to Him. Only then could the Kingdom expand in my life as He meant for it to do.

It's time ladies and gentlemen for many of us to move forward; for many of us to expand; for many of us to step out. It is time for us to come completely under the rule, the reign, the manifest presence of God, and yield our lives to the ever expanding, perpetually growing Kingdom of God. This is God's plan and purpose for your life—growth!

expanding, perpetually growing Kingdom of God. This is God's plan and purpose for your life—growth!

There's an interesting verse where Yeshua is talking with His disciples where He says to Peter, "Upon this rock I will build my church—my *ekkelsia*—and the gates of Hell shall not prevail against it." (Matt.16:18) Over the years I've heard many people use this verse to try to ward off the enemy from their lives.

When I hear someone say that, I always ask myself the question, "Have you ever seen a gate move? When does a gate attack?" Yeshua wasn't talking about defense; He was talking about offense! He was saying, "Take the gates of the enemy down. Not even the gates of Hell itself can prevail against you as you move forward." That is not a defensive verse!

It's time to believe God for greater

violence, and the violent take it by force." In this passage we see again the truth that the Kingdom of God is continually breaking forth, continually expanding. It has a forceful nature! There's a radical nature to this whole thing!

It is time for us to stop being passive, and declare "Revival," and "God use me." Today is the day for you to stand up and submit yourself to the perpetually expanding Kingdom of God! His plan is for your increase today.

My prayer of praise and victory for your life: *Hallelujah! Thank You for the victory, O God. Thank You that the battle is won! The battle has been won!!! The victory has been won! Move us forward, O God. The battle has been won! Your Kingdom is expanding. The battle is won! The victory is won! Move us forward God.*

Expand us, O God. Hallelujah! Thank You Lord. We submit ourselves to Your rule! We submit ourselves to Your reign, O God. Expand us O God! Expand those with one talent, expand those with five talents, and expand those with ten talents. Bring increase to Your people. Move us forward, O God. We break forth, O God. Revival is here, O God! Use us! Hallelujah!

In 1967, Evangelist Louis Kaplan began a simple 15 minute radio program called *Jewish Voice Broadcasts*, and the foundation was laid for a ministry that would grow to reach around the world to take the Gospel of Yeshua both to the Chosen People and to the Gentiles.

Over the past four decades, hundreds of thousands of Jews have come to faith in Yeshua as the Messiah through our various ministry outreaches. Whether it's providing free medical care at one of our clinics, using traditional Jewish music and dance at a *Hear O' Israel! Festival* to share the Gospel, training pastors and church leaders at one of our Bible Institutes, using television, radio and the

Internet to share the truth, or at one of our conferences, this ministry is dedicated to reaching people and meeting needs.

Since 1998, when Louis Kaplan went to Heaven, the ministry has been headed by Evangelist Jonathan Bernis. His vision has expanded the work of Jewish Voice around the world, resulting in a wonderful harvest of souls. The television program *Jewish Voice Today* is now seen in dozens of countries, including the nation of Israel. Rabbi Bernis is in great demand as a speaker on topics ranging such as Christian-Jewish relations, replacement theology, Middle East affairs, and Bible prophecy.

In 2007 as we celebrated our 40th year of ministry, the Lord provided us with the new Messianic Media Center. This state-of-the-art production facility will allow us to greatly improve both the quality and the quantity of our television programming, reaching more people with the Gospel through modern technology. We are excited about possibilities God is opening to us for future ministry around the world.